STECK-VAUGHN

PORTRAIT OF AMERICA

Washington

Steck-Vaughn Company

Executive Editor	Diane Sharpe
Senior Editor	Martin S. Saiewitz
Design Manager	Pamela Heaney
Photo Editor	Margie Foster
Electronic Cover Graphics	Alan Klemp

Proof Positive/Farrowlyne Associates, Inc.
Program Editorial, Revision Development, Design, and Production

Consultant: Carrie L. Wilkinson, Washington State Tourism

Published by Raintree Steck-Vaughn Publishers, an imprint of Steck-Vaughn Company.

A Turner Educational Services, Inc. book. Based on the Portrait of America television series by R. E. (Ted) Turner.

Cover Photo: Picture Lake by © Superstock.

Library of Congress Cataloging-in-Publication Data

Thompson, Kathleen.
  Washington / Kathleen Thompson.
    p.   cm. — (Portrait of America)
  "Based on the Portrait of America television series"—T.p. verso.
  "A Turner book."
  Includes index.
  ISBN 0-8114-7393-7 (library binding).—ISBN 0-8114-7474-7 (softcover)
    1. Washington (State)—Juvenile literature. [1. Washington (State)]
  I. Title. II. Series: Thompson, Kathleen. Portrait of America.
  F891.3.T48 1996
  979.7—dc20   95-25733
                                                         CIP
                                                         AC

Printed and Bound in the United States of America

4 5 6 7 8 9 10 WZ 03 02 01 00 99

Acknowledgments
The publishers wish to thank the following for permission to reproduce photographs:
P. 7 © Superstock; p. 8 © Robert Esposito/Panorama Designs; p. 10 Washington State Historical Society, Tacoma; p. 11 Mt. Baker Ranger District, North Cascades National Park, National Park Service; pp. 12, 13 (both), 14 Washington State Historical Society, Tacoma; p. 15 Bureau of Reclamation, U.S. Department of the Interior, Grand Coulee Project Office; p. 17 UPI/Bettmann; p. 18 (top) © Tim Haske/Profiles West, (bottom) © Don Wilson/Port of Seattle; p. 19 © Animals, Animals; p. 20 © The Seattle Times; p. 21 (top) © Josef Scaylea/The Seattle Times, (bottom) © Tom Reese/The Seattle Times; p. 22 Jim Huges/Mt. St. Helens National Volcanic Monument, USDA National Forest Service; pp. 23, 24 Mt. St. Helens National Volcanic Monument, USDA National Forest Service; p. 25 Jim Nieland/Mt. St. Helens National Volcanic Monument, USDA National Forest Service; p. 26 Boeing; p. 28 (top) © Michael Reagan, (bottom) Microsoft; p. 29 © Michael Reagan; p. 30 Washington Department of Agriculture; p. 31 (top) © Grant Heilman/Profiles West, (bottom) Public Utility District No. 1 of Douglas County; pp. 32, 33 © Larry J. Workman; p. 34 © Joel Rogers/Tony Stone Images; p. 36 (top) © Molly Morrow Photography, (bottom) © Patricia Ike/Tinowit Powwow; p. 37 (top) Makah Museum, (bottom) © Assunta Ng/Northwest Asian Weekly Foundation; p. 38 © Michael Reagan; p. 39 (top) © Mt. Rainier National Park, National Park Service, (bottom) © Allan Koss/MCA Records; p. 40 © Assunta Ng/Northwest Asian Weekly Foundation; p. 41 (top) © Assunta Ng/Northwest Asian Weekly Foundation, (bottom) © Randal Alhadeff; p. 42 © Michael J. Howell/Profiles West; p. 44 © Larry J. Workman; p. 46 One Mile Up; p. 47 (left) One Mile Up, (center) © William D. Bransford/National Wildflower Research Center, (right) © J. R. Woodward/Vireo.

STECK-VAUGHN

PORTRAIT OF AMERICA

Washington

Kathleen Thompson

A Turner Book

RAINTREE
STECK-VAUGHN
PUBLISHERS

The Steck-Vaughn Company

Austin, Texas

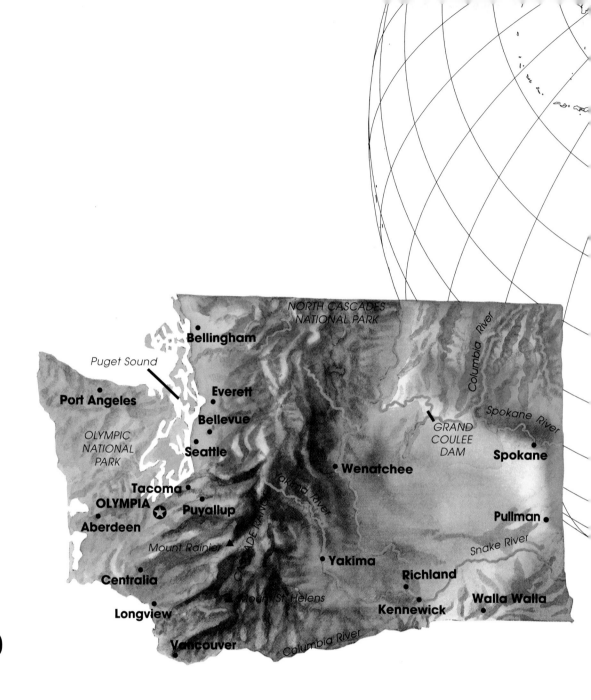

Washington

NORTH CASCADES
NATIONAL PARK

Puget Sound

Bellingham

Everett

Bellevue

Port Angeles

OLYMPIC
NATIONAL
PARK

Seattle

Columbia River

Spokane River

GRAND
COULEE
DAM

Spokane

Wenatchee

Tacoma

OLYMPIA

Puyallup

Yakima River

Pullman

Aberdeen

Mount Rainier

CASCADE RANGE

Snake River

Yakima

Richland

Centralia

Mount St. Helens

Walla Walla

Kennewick

Longview

Vancouver

Columbia River

Contents

Introduction

Washington, named for George Washington, truly reflects the character of its namesake. Like our first President, a farmer, Washington citizens make wise use of their state's abundant natural resources through farming, fishing, and logging. Like George Washington, a bold visionary, the people of Washington also believe in progress. Their state is home to the Grand Coulee Dam, one of the engineering wonders of the world. Washington produces aircraft and spacecraft for the United States military and NASA. No doubt President Washington would be proud of this great state, a center of agriculture, learning, and technology.

The Palouse Hills, a region of southeast Washington, has the world's most fertile dryland wheat farms.

Washington

unt Rainier, Puget Sound

Washington: Carved from the Timberland

Archaeologists believe that people have been living in present-day Washington for about nine thousand years. These ancient people survived mostly by fishing. Evidence of their society is found in artifacts such as weapons, tools, and drawings in caves and on cliff faces.

By 1775 as many as seventy different Native American groups lived in the area that would become Washington. Native Americans living west of the Cascade Mountains along the Pacific Ocean coast included Chinook, Clallam, Makah, Puyallup, and Snohomish. These people survived by fishing, trading, and gathering nuts and other vegetation. They built their homes and canoes from cedar trees, and they used the bark of cedar trees to make clothing.

The Cayuse, Nez Percé, Palouse, Spokane, and Yakima groups were living east of the Cascade Mountains. Most of these people fished from rivers instead of the ocean. They also hunted elk, moose, bighorn sheep, and deer. These Native Americans did

This ship is a replica of the one that brought Robert Gray and his crew to the mouth of the Columbia River in 1792. Gray named the river after his ship, the *Columbia*.

Captain George Vancouver and other early British explorers of the Pacific Northwest were sent to find the Northwest Passage, a western sea route from Europe to the Orient. None were ever successful because the only route that exists is a dangerous path near the North Pole.

not live in permanent villages but rather followed the migrations of the animals they hunted. Most dug shelters into the sides of hills or cliffs.

Around 1750 Russian fur traders settled in what is now Alaska. The Spanish, who had been exploring the Pacific Coast for almost two hundred years, were concerned that the Russians would move south into present-day Washington. As a result the Spanish sent several explorers to claim the area. Bruno de Heceta was the first of these. He arrived in present-day Washington in 1775. Later some of his crew were killed by a group of Native Americans.

British explorer Captain James Cook explored the coast in 1778. His attempts to land his ships were unsuccessful because of bad weather. Captain George Vancouver and his officer Peter Puget arrived with their crew in 1792 and mapped Puget Sound. Vancouver also named Mount Baker, Mount Rainier, and Mount St. Helens.

The first American to explore the area, Robert Gray, also arrived in 1792. Gray had been sent by a New England trading company to barter with the Native Americans. While he was there, he discovered the Columbia River. In 1804 President Thomas Jefferson sent Meriwether Lewis and William Clark to find a route to the Pacific Ocean. Their 1,700-mile trip began in St. Louis, Missouri, and ended at the mouth of the Columbia River in November 1805.

Soon fur traders from both the United States and Great Britain had set up trading posts all across what is now western Washington. The area became part of a vast territory called the Oregon Country, which included parts of present-day Washington, California, Oregon, Idaho, and Canada.

In 1818 the United States and Great Britain signed a treaty that allowed both countries to trade and settle in the Oregon Country. Traders were joined in the territory by missionaries who wanted to teach the Christian religion to Native Americans.

In 1836 Marcus and Narcissa Whitman established a mission near present-day Walla Walla, where the Cayuse lived. In addition to setting up a school, the Whitmans taught the Cayuse modern farming methods, such as irrigation, and helped them build European-style houses.

In 1847 a measles epidemic broke out at the Whitmans' mission, and many Cayuse died. Believing that the Whitmans had poisoned them, the Cayuse attacked the mission and killed the Whitmans along

Mount Baker was formed about 500,000 years ago, when volcanoes along the Cascade Mountains spewed lava and ash for long periods of time.

with 15 other mission residents. This incident was the beginning of many clashes that erupted between settlers and Native Americans in the area.

American settlers began arriving in greater numbers when the Oregon Trail opened around 1843. The trail was a pioneer route that began in Missouri and ended at two points—Fort Vancouver and Oregon City. Soon American settlers began to outnumber British traders in the Oregon Country. The settlers, along with many other people across the nation, believed that the United States shouldn't have to share the area with Great Britain. In 1844 James K. Polk ran for President under the slogan "Fifty-four Forty or Fight." Polk's phrase meant that he intended to gain all of the territory below the latitude of 54°40' for the United States. If Great Britain wouldn't agree to this, Polk was ready to send American troops into war.

Polk was elected and immediately set to work on peaceful negotiations with Great Britain. In 1846 Congress signed a treaty with Great Britain called the Oregon Boundary Treaty. The treaty set the border between the United States and Canada at the 49th parallel—quite a bit lower than Polk's public position. The newly defined area was officially named the Oregon Territory in 1848.

In 1853 Congress created the Washington Territory, which included all of present-day Washington as well as parts of Idaho and Montana. The governor of the new territory, Isaac Ingalls Stevens, wanted more land for American settlers. He asked many Native American groups to sign treaties

Isaac Ingalls Stevens was the first territorial governor of Washington. Stevens began the displacement of Native Americans in the area onto reservations.

greeing to move to reservations. Some of the groups signed the treaties, but many saw no reason to move from the land that had been their home for years. A Yakima chief named Kamiakin led many of these Native American groups in attacks on the settlers. But diseases such as cholera, smallpox, and measles weakened and killed many Native Americans. In 1858 Kamiakin and his followers were defeated and moved to reservations.

In 1863 Congress created the Idaho Territory, which defined the present boundaries of Washington. The Northern Pacific Railroad, the first railroad line to the Northwest, reached Tacoma in 1883, bringing more settlers than ever before. By the late 1880s, the population of the Washington Territory reached well over three hundred thousand. On November 11, 1889, Washington became the forty-second state, with Olympia as its capital.

Washington was a busy state. The logging industry was thriving, and by around 1900 thousands of Washington's workers were lumberjacks. In addition, farmers began to irrigate the dry land of eastern Washington. Many new crops—especially apples— were harvested and shipped across the country. Salmon

Kamiakin, chief of the Yakima, organized an army of almost two thousand Native Americans from many different groups. They waged war against settlers and the United States government.

Farming in the state began to boom during the 1890s, when irrigation was introduced to farms in eastern Washington.

13

fishing and coal mining also boosted Washington's growing economy. When gold was discovered in Alaska and Canada in 1897, Seattle became the place where northbound prospectors bought their supplies.

In 1909 Seattle hosted the Alaska-Yukon-Pacific Exposition. The exposition celebrated the gold rush in the north as well as Seattle's rapid economic growth. The state was still booming in 1917 when the United States became involved in World War I. The war raised the need for products from Washington, such as lumber and wheat. Shipbuilding factories in Puget Sound expanded their production. In addition, the Boeing Company, a new arrival to Seattle in 1916, increased its production of aircraft for the war.

After the war, however, Washington's economic situation took a turn for the worse. People who had been hired during the war now had to be laid off as production levels returned to normal. In fact, many people who had been working before the war had to be

The 1909 Alaska-Yukon-Pacific Exposition in Seattle attracted over 3.7 million people. President William Taft attended and gave a speech.

laid off, too. Those who still had jobs started protesting what they considered to be unfair labor practices by employers. The workers formed organizations called labor unions. These unions started protests, or strikes, in which workers halted production until their employers agreed to help solve their difficulties.

Grand Coulee Dam is the largest concrete dam in the United States.

Workers in Seattle organized a large general strike in February 1919. Almost sixty thousand workers left their jobs. After a few days some agreements were reached, and many people returned to work.

In the 1930s the whole nation suffered from an economic slump called the Great Depression. Companies involved in the state's major industries, especially logging and farming, were forced to cut production or close down entirely. About one third of Washington's workers lost their jobs.

To put Washington's unemployed back to work, the federal government began programs to build roads, plant trees, and, most importantly, build dams. Construction started on the Bonneville Dam in 1933 and the Grand Coulee Dam in 1936. The Grand Coulee alone put about seven thousand people in Washington back to work. In addition, both dams harnessed the water power of the Columbia River. Not only did the water power provide electricity to the area, the dams also encouraged new businesses. Water from the dams also helped to irrigate over one million acres of land in central Washington, and new farms began to thrive.

The state got another push forward when the United States entered World War II after Japanese forces bombed Pearl Harbor in Hawaii in 1941. Washington's farms produced food for troops overseas. Its factories manufactured ships, trucks, and railroad cars. The Boeing Company once again stepped up its airplane production. In addition, a nuclear energy center, the Hanford Works, was built in 1943. It was part of the Manhattan Project, the secret government project to build the first atomic bomb.

Because the United States was at war with Japan, the government was afraid that people of Japanese descent would spy on America's government and military. So, beginning in 1942, the government arranged to move all of the nation's Japanese Americans—over 13,000 in Washington alone—to relocation camps. When these innocent people were released at the end of the war three years later, most of them had lost their jobs, their homes, and their possessions. Some returned to Japan, disillusioned that the "land of the free" had imprisoned them for no good reason. Most started over again in the United States.

After the war more farmland was irrigated. Dams were built on Washington's rivers, producing energy for new industries. The aircraft industry in Washington, especially the Boeing Company, enjoyed huge profits. In 1959 a Boeing 707 flew nonstop to London from Seattle for the first time. The state's economy was thriving, but much of its success was dependent on Boeing.

In 1962 the Century 21 World's Fair was held in Seattle. It was the first World's Fair held in the United States since 1939. It brought almost ten million tourists to the state and created many modern-day landmarks such as the Space Needle and the monorail.

The late 1960s brought another economic slump to Washington, caused mainly by decreasing airplane sales. In the early 1960s, nearly sixty thousand people in the state worked for Boeing. But ten years later, almost forty thousand of these workers had been laid off. The economy picked up again when Boeing began to build more commercial aircraft in the 1970s. But the state soon realized that it needed to attract other industries so that one company wouldn't dominate its economy.

In 1974 Spokane hosted a world's fair called Expo '74. A major redevelopment program was put into effect to get the city ready. Millions of tourists came to the fair, which created an economic boom for Spokane residents.

This Japanese American woman and her children are being relocated by the United States Army from their home in Bainbridge Island, Washington, to California during World War II. The children are wearing army identification tags.

Olympic National Park extends over 896,599 acres, stretching inland from the coast of the Pacific Ocean.

A container ship is being loaded at the Port of Seattle.

In 1980 Washington faced a crisis. Mount St. Helens had been a silent volcano for 123 years. On May 18 it erupted, pouring debris and ash over southwestern Washington and nearby states. Some ash even reached as far east as Montana. Fifty-seven people and countless animals were killed. Billions of dollars' worth of property was damaged.

Heavy logging in Washington's forests throughout the twentieth century has also caused serious environmental problems. Many species of animals that live in and around forests, such as the spotted owl, are in danger of becoming extinct. The United States government banned much of the logging in Washington's forests in 1990. This ban helped protect the environment and endangered species, but it also put thousands of loggers out of work.

Washington is frequently ranked as one of the most pleasant states in the country. Perhaps the reason is because of its wide variety of landscapes and natural beauty. Washington has spectacular mountains, miles of ocean beaches, and acres of forests. Washington's beautiful surroundings also include a variety of resources—rivers and lakes, minerals, lumber, fish, and fertile soil. Preserving the surroundings and natural resources is important to Washington's citizens. That is why Washington has set aside large parcels of land for wildlife habitats, parks, and wilderness areas. Washington also has a thorough recycling program that helps to keep the environment clean. In addition, the state relies heavily on renewable energy resources, such as hydroelectric power from dams. Hydroelectric power is clean energy; it doesn't pollute or use up water. It also doesn't pollute the air.

Washington's population grew enormously during the 1990s, especially in the urban areas. Many of the cities' services were able to handle the heavy increase of people. Public transportation and public safety, for example, kept pace with the added demands. However, one problem that did occur is water pollution due to overworked waste treatment plants. Another is the increase in air pollution caused by the number of additional transport vehicles such as cars and buses.

Washington offers a high quality of life; it has modern cities, natural splendor, and a strong economy. Washington is dedicated to protecting the environment. Balancing the needs of its citizens with those of nature will be an ongoing challenge in the twenty-first century.

Washington's spotted owl is an endangered species.

Taking an Active Stand

Lake Washington in Seattle is a twenty-mile stretch of clear, blue water used for swimming, fishing, sailing, waterskiing, and enjoying cool summer breezes. Around 1950, people in the Seattle area began to notice that their lake wasn't as clear as it used to be. The city and surrounding communities had to close many beaches, having found the lake too dirty for safe swimming. To make matters worse, increased levels of algae fed by the lake's pollution began to give the area a horrible stench.

By 1958, when this photograph was taken, sewage from 14 cities drained into Lake Washington, making it too polluted for swimming.

As Seattle's population grew, Lake Washington continued to get worse. By 1955 nearly twenty million gallons of sewage were being dumped into the lake each day! At last someone decided to do something. A Seattle lawyer named Jim Ellis wanted his city to be a place where the quality of life was as important as the strength of the economy. He started a crusade in Seattle and in the 13 other cities that border Lake Washington.

Seattle-area activists set to work raising public support. "On one night," remembered Ellis, "we had five thousand mothers marching to make the lake safe for swimming. It was a major public effort." At last, in September 1958, the Seattle area voted to form a council to clean up their lake. They called the group the Municipality of Metropolitan Seattle— "Metro" for short.

Metro developed a cleanup plan and began making progress in 1961. Raw sewage was diverted to underground pipes that led to new treatment plants on nearby Puget Sound. The project cost $125 million, but it was well worth it. Within ten years all of Lake Washington's beaches were reopened. The people of the Seattle area had set an example for the entire nation. As Ellis said in a 1966 speech, "Ten years ago, the urban drainage basins of the nation were heavily polluted. Today, most of these waters have gone from bad to worse—but not here. . . . Today, most local councils are still waiting for someone else to do it—but not here."

The Seattle community continues working for Lake Washington. Metro council has begun a one-billion-dollar upgrade of the water treatment plants on Puget Sound. In addition to improving the water quality on the Sound, the upgraded plants will clean and recycle the water's wastes so that they can be used as fertilizer for farms and forests.

When Jim Ellis began practicing law in 1949, several small sewer districts around Lake Washington were his first clients.

Seattle has more to be proud of than just a clean lake. Its community dedication and cooperation serve as a model for other troubled cities now and in the years to come.

Today Lake Washington is safe for swimming and other water activities.

Nature Rebuilds Itself

Until 1980, people in southwest Washington thought of Mount St. Helens as just a peaceful, snow-topped mountain. The mountain had been quiet for 123 years. Nobody could remember the last time it had erupted. It was easy to forget that Mount St. Helens was a sleeping, or dormant, volcano.

Scientists who were studying the volcano, however, were worried. Mount St. Helens is in the Ring of Fire, which is made up of the land areas around the edges of the Pacific Ocean. The Ring of Fire has many volcanic eruptions and earthquakes. In 1975 scientists classified Mount St. Helens as one of the volcanoes that was most likely to erupt before the end of the century.

During March and April of 1980, Mount St. Helens gave Washington residents their first warnings that the volcano would erupt soon. The earth in southwest Washington shook, and several bursts of ash and steam erupted from the volcano. Most alarm-ing, Mount St. Helens began to swell and bulge on its north face. The bulge was caused by the movement of gas and liquid rock, called magma, into the volcano from deep inside the earth. The bulge moved about five feet each day. People who lived in the area were asked to leave for their own safety.

At 8:32 A.M. on May 18, there was a medium-sized earthquake just below the volcano. Within seconds, the bulged peak of Mount St. Helens collapsed in a huge avalanche. More than one thousand feet of mountain-top tumbled toward the nearby Toutle

Meta Lake is shown here surrounded by volcano-blasted timber. The blast of air that flattened these trees spewed ash and stone over 12 miles away.

The eruption of Mount St. Helens on May 18, 1980, was one of the biggest volcanic eruptions recorded in North American history.

River valley at speeds of 155 to 180 miles per hour. The landslide was the largest in recorded history.

The landslide uncorked the volcano. A blast of hot gas exploded out of the volcano's side. The explosion was heard in four states as well as in British Columbia, Canada. The blast was so strong that it destroyed everything within eight miles of the volcano. All the trees in this area were uprooted and sent flying at speeds of 220 to 670 miles per hour.

Within 19 miles of the volcano, all the trees were knocked down. Any trees left standing beyond this area were burned and killed. The landslide, together with the volcano's enormous blast, caused most of the destruction that day.

Shortly after the eruption, lava and broken rock emerged from Mount St. Helens's crest and spilled down the mountainside at 450 miles per hour. The lava was so hot that it measured over 700 degrees Fahrenheit two weeks later! On the opposite side of the volcano, hot mud poured down the mountainside.

Ten minutes after the blast, a 12-mile-high, mushroom-shaped cloud of ash had formed above Mount St.

This photo was taken of Meta Lake in 1984, four years after the devastation caused by the Mount St. Helens eruption. Many plants grew back quickly, but trees take much longer to grow.

Helens. It made the skies in eastern Washington so dark that streetlights had to be turned on during the afternoon. Two days later ash from the eruption was found on the East Coast, far to the other side of the country. Two weeks later ash from the volcano reached the other side of the world.

The Mount St. Helens eruption was the most destructive volcanic disaster in the history of the United States. Fifty-seven people died, most by suffocating in the gas from the blast. Tens of thousands of acres of forest were destroyed. Most elk, deer, bears, birds, and medium-sized animals in the area were killed. Many small animals, such as frogs and mice, survived because they were underground or underwater at the time of the blast.

Because of the incredible destruction, scientists thought that the environment would take decades to recover. However, nature provides a way to rebuild itself. Mount St. Helens's ash and lava contained many minerals that helped to enrich the soil. Also, the volcano's blast only destroyed what was above the ground. New plants quickly began to grow from underground root systems that were left unharmed. Wildlife returned to the area to feed on the new vegetation.

Forestry companies pitched in to harvest the downed trees and plant new ones. In less than a decade, the Mount St. Helens environment was thriving again.

Mount St. Helens remained active in the decade after the 1980 eruption. There were earthquakes, and the volcano developed dramatic new bulges of magma and gas. Sometimes Mount St. Helens erupted explosively, which frightened local residents. Some of these eruptions formed nine-mile-high ash columns above the volcano.

But none of these events were as devastating as the May 18, 1980, eruption.

Scientists don't know when Mount St. Helens will return to its slumber. But they do know this: Mount St. Helens has a fifty-thousand-year history. That means the mountain is young for a volcano. Whether Mount St. Helens sleeps for two hundred years or two thousand years, it will reawaken. When that happens, anyone living nearby would be wise to remember the events of May 18, 1980.

The peaceful beauty of Mount St. Helens before the eruption is shown here overlooking Bear Cove.

An Airborne Economy

Airplanes are Washington's single largest industry. Well over one hundred thousand of the nearly two million workers in the state build aircraft. One company, Boeing, employs nearly three quarters of all these aerospace workers. Boeing is a highly successful company. It is one of the largest manufacturers of commercial airplanes in the world.

Although Boeing does well most of the time, it has had bad years. When Boeing is doing well, there are a lot of jobs in Washington. When Boeing's production falls off—as it did in the early 1970s—many people are out of work. These unemployed people can't afford to eat at restaurants, go to the movies, or buy new clothes or cars. That means that when Boeing lays off employees, other Washington businesses suffer as well.

That's why Washington is working to create more varied industry in the state. The second most important manufacturing industry in Washington is food processing. Most of Washington's food industry workers preserve and can fruits, vegetables, and fish,

Boeing has been one of the world's largest commercial airplane manufacturers for more than thirty years.

Washington's forestry industry raises about two hundred million dollars for the state each year.

As the leader of Microsoft, Bill Gates is one of the most influential people in the computer industry.

especially salmon. Some of them also mill flour or package meat and dairy products.

Washington's forest resources make wood products the state's third largest manufacturing activity. Mills and factories process trees to produce lumber, plywood, and shingles.

One rapidly growing area of manufacturing in Washington is computer software. The company that is mainly responsible for this development is Microsoft Corporation, based in Redmond. Microsoft was started in 1975 by a Seattle native, Bill Gates, when he was only 19 years old. Today Microsoft is the largest software company in the world.

Even more important to Washington than manufacturing, however, are service industries. Service industries are those in which people don't manufacture an actual product. Instead, they may work at a department store, a bank, or an insurance company. All of Washington's service industries taken together bring in almost $35 billion each year.

The most important category of service industries in Washington is business and community services, which includes law firms, hospitals, and personnel service companies. Most of these businesses are based in urban areas such as Seattle and Tacoma. Washington's pioneering health care system has made health care institutions especially important to the state economy.

The manufacturing of wood products employs about 55,000 of Washington's workers. This photo shows red cedars being transported for processing.

The second largest category of service industries in the state is wholesale and retail trade. Wholesale trade involves the buying and selling of large quantities of products to businesses. Washington's many ports have made wholesale trade especially important, as the state's goods are shipped to businesses across the globe. Retail trade involves the buying and selling of small quantities of goods to individuals, such as new clothes, a car, or the week's groceries. One retail trade business that has become important to Washington is Starbucks Coffee. Incorporated in Seattle in 1992, Starbucks employs about six thousand service workers nationwide. In all, Washington has almost six hundred thousand workers in wholesale and retail trade. They help bring in almost half of the state's income.

The tourist industry, an important part of Washington's economy, also employs many service workers. These people may work at information centers, museums, restaurants, or souvenir shops.

All tourism-related jobs taken together employ the fourth-largest number of workers in the state. Tourists spend well over $7.2 billion in Washington each year.

The bustle of its urban areas makes many people forget that Washington is one of the top farming states in the nation. In fact, the production of about twenty of Washington's crops ranks either first, second, or third in the nation. Most of Washington's farms are east of the Cascade Mountains. Much of this land used to be desert, but dams and irrigation have turned it into good farmland. Nearly half of Washington's more than 35,000 farms are irrigated.

Washington's most important crop is apples. In fact, Washington has been the nation's number-one producer of apples since the 1920s. Currently the state produces about five billion pounds of apples each year! Washington is also the nation's number one producer of sweet cherries, Concord grapes, red raspberries, and lentils. Production of potatoes, pears, and apricots ranks second in the nation, while green peas and sweet corn come in third. Although Washington may not be on the top of the nation's list of wheat producers, wheat is still the state's most valuable field crop, bringing in over $450 million each year.

Other important agricultural products, such as beef cattle, horses, and sheep, are raised mostly in the eastern part of the state. Washington also has

Flowers and other nursery products are important to Washington's economy, bringing in over $160 million a year.

many dairy farms in the western part of the state, and milk is a valuable farm product.

Washington also has plenty of natural resources to help its economy. Forests, fish, and minerals are very important to the state's economy. Alaska is the only state in the nation where more salmon are caught than in Washington. As for mining, Washington has more coal than any other state on the West Coast. Gravel, gold, silver, magnesium, zinc, and other minerals bring mining's total yearly income to over $325 million.

Washington may be well-known for its airplanes, but it was natural resources that first made its economy successful. Few states have the abundant resources that Washington has. The people of this state, however, are trying to be careful not to use too many of their resources too quickly. If Washington can expand its economic resources as it conserves its natural ones, its economy will continue to flourish.

Washington produces more apples than any other state. In 1989, Washington's Centennial year, legislators named the apple Washington's state fruit.

Dams are crucial to Washington's economy, supplying hydroelectric power for thousands of businesses.

Salmon and the Quinault

The Quinault in Washington are one of the nation's few Native American groups that haven't been displaced by the federal government. But that doesn't mean that their lives haven't changed. Since their reservation was created in 1855, the Quinault have gone through many struggles to preserve their way of life. One of the biggest struggles has been to maintain the amount of sockeye salmon available to them. The sockeye salmon has been one of the Quinault's main sources of food and income for generations.

Quinault means "canoe people," a name they acquired centuries ago when they fished from cedar canoes. For generations the Quinault have taken care of Lake Quinault and the Quinault River, where the salmon thrive. They knew that if they caught too many fish, there would be fewer for the next year. So they monitored their catch carefully. As Joe De La Cruz, a former president of the Quinault Indian Nation, explained, "It's more or less ingrained in our people that we

Sockeye salmon are one of the main sources of income for the Quinault.

have to take care of things that are provided for us or there's not going to be anything for future generations."

In 1970 the Quinault began to notice that overfishing and pollution from outside sources had diminished the number of sockeye salmon. As a result, they organized the Quinault Resources Development Project. The people involved in the project—which also works to protect the area's forests and wildlife—spent a number of years counting the salmon. They also analyzed the water quality of Lake Quinault and the Quinault River. They worked to protect the areas of the river that the sockeye inhabited. They also built hatcheries, which are safe places for fish to lay their eggs. Today about two million fish are raised in the hatcheries each year. Then they are released to breed in the wild. In addition, the project works with other fishing organizations in the Pacific Northwest to make sure that government policy continues to preserve the salmon and their environment.

The Quinault continue to work with the government to keep Lake Quinault and the Quinault River

healthy and stocked with salmon. As Joe De La Cruz explained, "The preservation of the Pacific salmon and the enhancement of [their habitat]—it just totally ties with our society, our culture, our heritage. Without the salmon, we'd be another displaced generation or displaced people, like a lot of displaced people in the world."

Joe De La Cruz, former president of the Quinault Indian Nation, speaks on the preservation of Quinault fishing culture.

Washington Way of Life

Washington is a relatively young state, but its cultural history goes back further than that of some of the first states in the nation. Artifacts discovered at Marmes Rockshelter in eastern Washington are some of the oldest artifacts in the Western Hemisphere. Rock paintings drawn by early civilizations can be found in caves and on cliff sides across the state.

The Ozette archaeological site on the Olympic Coast has yielded many drawings and carvings that are about five hundred years old. The most spectacular discovery from this site is a life-size wooden carving of a whale fin studded with the teeth of otters.

The state's many museums, as well as its cultural events, display the traditions of Washington's ancestors. More than eighty thousand Native Americans host festivals and powwows across the state that people of all backgrounds can enjoy. In addition, the Thomas Burke Memorial Museum explores the histories of the many Native American groups of the Pacific Northwest. The state's 250,000 Hispanic residents host

In the Pacific Northwest, some Native American groups carve their family symbols, or totems, on totem poles. This one stands in Seattle's Pioneer Square.

The Ellensburg Rodeo, held every Labor Day, features Native American dancing in addition to standard rodeo events.

In Yakima every June, Native American dancers and drummers from all over the United States and Canada celebrate at the Tinowit International Pow Wow.

celebrations for the Mexican holiday Cinco de Mayo, and both Native Americans and Hispanics hold rodeos virtually year-round. The cultures of Washington's 250,000 Asian Americans are represented by the Seattle Art Museum's remarkable collection of Asian art. Much of this art has been obtained through the state's continuing trade with countries across the Pacific. In addition, German Volksmarches, Scottish Highland Games, and Scandinavian Viking Fests celebrate the cultural histories of some of Washington's older European communities.

Washington has several symphony orchestras. The Seattle Symphony Orchestra, established in 1903, is one of the finest in the nation. The Seattle Repertory Theater is nationally acclaimed, and the Seattle Opera Association has received international recognition, especially for its presentations of operas by Richard Wagner. In addition, many future actors graduate from the school of drama at the University of Washington, one of the nation's first university drama schools.

Washington's cultural resources have encouraged some of our nation's finest artists. One example is dancer and choreographer Robert Joffrey. Born in Seattle, Joffrey grew up well aware of Washington's cultural diversity. His parents were both immigrants, one from Afghanistan and the other from Italy. Joffrey first learned dance, both tap and ballet, in Seattle. He later moved to New York City and established one of the nation's most innovative modern dance companies, the Joffrey Ballet, in 1956. What made this company so special was Joffrey's willingness to incorporate both old and new dance forms into every production. Robert Joffrey died in 1988, but his

The artifacts at the Ozette site were particularly well preserved because they had been buried in a mud slide.

Chinese New Year is celebrated every year in late January or early February in Seattle's International District.

37

company still carries on the established tradition of blending classical ballet with modern dance.

Another Washington innovator was architect Minoru Yamasaki. Born in Seattle in 1912, Yamasaki graduated from the University of Washington and went on to become one of the nation's most famous architects. He designed more than three hundred buildings across the nation and around the world, all of which challenged traditional architectural forms. His most famous structure, the World Trade Center in New York City, was completed in 1972. Its distinctive twin towers are among the tallest in the world. Yamasaki died in 1986.

Also born in Seattle in 1912, Mary McCarthy became one of the nation's most outspoken writers. Her novels wittily address many issues, especially women's roles in American society. Her most famous books include *The Group* and *Memories of a Catholic Girlhood*. McCarthy also helped run one of the nation's most prominent literary journals, the *Partisan Review*.

Washington has also produced its share of talented musicians. One of the first to gain worldwide recognition was Bing Crosby. Born in Tacoma in 1903, Crosby began singing while he was at law school in Spokane. His first popular success came with his role in the 1931 movie *King of Jazz*. Crosby's recording of "White Christmas" is still one of the best-selling records ever.

It was Crosby's soft, crooning voice that made him popular. Many other Washington natives, however, especially those from Seattle, have gained popularity for producing very different kinds of sounds. The first

Washington's Olympic Peninsula has one of the only rain forests in the United States.

of Seattle's alternative musical stars was Jimi Hendrix. Born in 1942, Hendrix taught himself to play guitar in high school. He soon began using his guitar to create sounds and styles that no one had ever heard. Songs such as "Purple Haze" and his own arrangement of the "Star-Spangled Banner" made Hendrix a symbol of the counterculture in the 1960s.

Jimi Hendrix died at age 27, but the impact he made on rock music in that short time is still being felt today. Many of Seattle's more recent rock stars cite Hendrix as a major influence. These musicians include bands such as Nirvana, Pearl Jam, and Soundgarden, founders of the "grunge" style that swept rock music in the 1990s.

Washington's culture is as much a product of its many different ethnic backgrounds as its innovation and energy. What Washington artists can claim is the unique experience that living in Washington brings to their creativity.

Jimi Hendrix was famous for his improvised solos on the electric guitar.

Success Story

Traditionally most Chinese girls were raised to lead quiet lives as wives and mothers. But Assunta Ng had other ideas for her future. Assunta Ng left her home in Hong Kong to come to Washington when she was 18 years old. Her father agreed to support her while she studied at the University of Washington, in Seattle, for one year. But when that year was up, Assunta didn't return home to raise a family. Instead she earned a scholarship and took on three part-time jobs to support herself.

Assunta was pleased with the active Asian-American community she found in Seattle. But she noticed that it was missing something very important. "I remember one time when I read about Thomas Jefferson," she said. "He was asked, 'Which is more important, the government or a newspaper?' And he chose the newspaper. . . . Once you don't have a newspaper in the community, everybody just goes blind."

In 1982, only eight years after her college graduation, Assunta published the first issue of the *Seattle Chinese Post*. There hadn't been a Chinese newspaper in the community since 1927. "Our people relied on rumors, gossip. And I wanted our people to read facts," said Assunta, remembering her determination in the paper's

Most of Seattle's Asian-American residents live in the International District. Seattle's Asian Americans are mainly descended from Chinese, Japanese, Filipino, and Korean immigrants.

Assunta Ng is the founder of the Seattle Chinese Post.

the focus of the English edition. But most welcomed the change, realizing the strength in such diversity. As Assunta Ng and editor Susan L. Cassidy wrote for the first expanded edition, "While there is much to be gained by valuing the distinctions, there is also a great deal to be gained by uniting the various Asian groups. . . . There is strength in numbers."

Assunta Ng also realizes the strength of her membership in the American community. "I'm still a Chinese," she said, "and within me I carry five thousand years of history and culture, and that has to be shared. . . . I'm Chinese, but I also live in America. I am Chinese-American."

Assunta Ng and three staff members put out the first 12-page issue of the *Post* from a tiny office with a borrowed typewriter and no copier machine. Today the twenty-member *Post* staff puts out a 32-page Chinese edition and a 20-page English edition each week. Assunta Ng and the paper both have won countless local and national awards. The English edition is now called *Northwest Asian Weekly* in order to include other members of the area's Asian community.

Some of the paper's Chinese read-ers didn't like her decision to expand

These are issues of the Seattle Chinese Post (with text in Chinese) and the Northwest Asian Weekly.

A Place of Possibilities

Washington is a place of possibilities. For example, Washington has the most potential waterpower of any state in the nation, but more than half of that waterpower is still untapped. More hydroelectric power would mean more electricity for businesses and cities. Although the state has already turned more than a million acres of desert into productive farms, there are still large areas of land in the center of the state that could be reclaimed.

While some resources aren't used enough, others—like the state's forests—are overused. Too much logging causes erosion, which muddies rivers. It also ruins the habitats of threatened or endangered species such as the spotted owl and the bald eagle.

Endangered species and natural environments are also being hurt by pollution. Washington has led the nation in creative solutions to environmental problems, and it now maintains some of the strictest pollution standards in the nation. Many businesses argue,

Seattle's Space Needle symbolizes Washington's optimism about the future. It was built in 1962 for the Century 21 World's Fair.

The fact that such beautiful, unspoiled scenes still exist in Washington provides hope that the state will be able to maintain its high standards of environmental protection.

however, that these standards are so strict that they discourage economic growth.

The state adopted a new health care system in May 1994. Under this plan residents and their employers pay for half of the people's health care, and the state government pays for the other half. Washington's health care plan is so practical that it has been used as a model by other states and even by the federal government.

It's going to take wisdom to guard nature and build stable industries while continuing to preserve the quality of life in the state. Washington's citizens have proved themselves among the most active and dedicated in the nation. With citizens like that, the possibilities for the state of Washington are truly endless.

Important Historical Events

1592 Juan de Fuca claims the discovery of the strait that bears his name.

1775 Spanish explorer Bruno de Heceta arrives in present-day Washington.

1778 Captain James Cook explores the coast of present-day Washington.

1792 George Vancouver and Peter Puget survey Puget Sound. Robert Gray sails into Gray Harbor.

1805 The expedition of Meriwether Lewis and William Clark reaches the mouth of the Columbia River at the Pacific Ocean in November.

1818 Great Britain and the United States sign a treaty that allows citizens of both countries to settle and to trade in the Oregon Territory.

1836 Marcus and Narcissa Whitman establish a medical mission near today's Walla Walla.

1843 The Oregon Trail opens, bringing settlers into the Washington area.

1846 The United States and Great Britain sign the Oregon Boundary Treaty, setting Washington's northern border at the forty-ninth parallel.

1848 Congress officially forms the Oregon Territory, which includes present-day Washington.

1853 Congress forms the Washington Territory. Governor Isaac Ingalls Stevens begins trying to move Native Americans onto reservations. Native American wars and raids on settlers begin.

1858 Native American wars end with the defeat of the Yakima chief Kamiakin.

1883 The Northern Pacific Railroad reaches Tacoma.

1889 Washington becomes the forty-second state in November.

1897 The Klondike and Alaska gold rushes begin. Seattle becomes a supply center for miners.

1909 The Alaska-Yukon-Pacific Exposition is held in Seattle.

1916 The Boeing Company begins to manufacture airplanes in Seattle.

1919 Sixty thousand workers in Seattle go on strike in February to protest layoffs.

1933 Construction begins on the Bonneville Dam.

1942 The Grand Coulee Dam is completed.

1942 Japanese Americans in Washington are moved to relocation camps.

1943 The Hanford Works helps to make the first atomic bomb.

1958 "Metro" is formed in Seattle to clean up Lake Washington.

1959 A Boeing 707 completes the first nonstop flight from Seattle to London.

1962 The Century 21 World's Fair opens in Seattle.

1974 Spokane hosts the Expo '74 World's Fair.

1975 Bill Gates establishes the Microsoft Corporation.

1980 Mount St. Helens erupts, killing 57 people and causing billions of dollars' worth of damage.

1990 The federal government limits logging in Washington forests.

1994 Washington adopts a new health care system, one of the most comprehensive in the nation.

Washington's flag shows the state seal, a portrait of George Washington, for whom the state is named. The portrait is encircled with a yellow band in the middle of a dark green background, which symbolizes Washington's forests.

Washington Almanac

Nickname. The Evergreen State

Capital. Olympia

State Bird. Willow goldfinch or wild canary

State Flower. Coast rhododendron

State Tree. Western hemlock

State Motto. *Alki* ("Bye and Bye")

State Song. "Washington, My Home"

State Abbreviations. Wash. (traditional); WA (postal)

Statehood. November 11, 1889, the 42nd state

Government. Congress: U.S. senators, 2; U.S. representatives, 9. State Legislature: senators, 49; representatives, 98. Counties: 39

Area. 68,126 sq mi (176,446 sq km), 20th in size among the states

Greatest Distances. north/south, 239 mi (385 km); east/west, 370 mi (595 km). Coastline: 157 mi (253 km)

Elevation. Highest: Mount Rainier, 14,410 ft (4,392 m). Lowest: sea level, along the Pacific Ocean

Population. 1990 Census: 4,887,941 (18% increase over 1980), 18th in population among the states. Density: 72 persons per sq mi (28 persons per sq km). Distribution: 76% urban, 24% rural. 1980 Census: 4,132,204

Economy. *Agriculture:* apples, wheat, cherries, grapes, raspberries, lentils, potatoes, nursery and greenhouse products, apricots, pears, beef cattle, dairy products, timber. *Fishing:* salmon, oysters, shrimp, crabs, trout. *Manufacturing:* transportation products, processed food products, lumber and wood products. *Mining:* coal, gravel, silver, magnesium, zinc

State Seal

State Flower:
Coast rhododendron

State Bird: Willow goldfinch or
wild canary

Annual Events

★ Northwest Trek Volksmarch in Eatonville (February)

★ Cherry Blossom and Japanese Cultural Festival in Seattle (April)

★ Cinco de Mayo celebration in Pasco (May)

★ International Children's Festival in Seattle (May)

★ Tinowit International Pow Wow in Yakima (June)

★ Seafair in Seattle (July/August)

★ Chief Seattle Days in Suquamish (August)

★ Ellensburg Rodeo in Ellensburg (September)

★ Western Washington State Fair in Puyallup (September)

★ Wenatchee River Salmon Festival in Wenatchee (October)

Places to Visit

★ Bavarian Village in Leavenworth

★ Eagle Sanctuary, near Concrete

★ Frontier Village in Winthrop

★ Grand Coulee Dam, west of Spokane

★ Mount Rainier National Park

★ Mount St. Helens National Volcanic Monument, near Toutle

★ Pacific Science Center and the Space Needle in Seattle

★ San Juan Islands in Puget Sound

★ Washington State History Museum in Tacoma

★ Whitman Mission National Historic Site

Index